the journey

The Mission of Jesus

The Gospel of John (Chapters 12–21)

Charles "Chic" Shaver

BEACON HILL PRESS
OF KANSAS CITY

Contents

1

Strange Happenings
John 12:1-19; 16:16-33

Prayer

Begin your Bible study with a brief prayer. Ask God to open your hearts and to help you understand His Word.

Opening Thoughts

Usually at the end of a book or movie, the story begins to wrap itself up neatly. Confusing things become clear, and mysteries are solved. Everyone finally sees the big picture. That's not so in the case of Jesus. The last week of the earthly life of Jesus must have been extremely important to John because he devoted one-third of his Gospel to it.

Although Jesus' days on earth never came anywhere close to normalcy, the last week or so just seemed to grow increasingly strange. He's dining with a previously dead man, He's being anointed with expensive perfume, He's taking celebratory rides into town on a donkey, He's telling His disciples that He'll be leaving without them, and He's warning His followers that they will be hated. As He stooped to wash the disciples' feet (an act usually only done by a servant) or told some of them they would betray Him or deny Him, you have to wonder if the disciples were confused and worried about the days to come.

Discuss the Scripture

Read John 12:1-11

1. In John 11:17-45 Mary and Martha's brother, Lazarus, had died and then was brought back to life by Jesus. How does this put Mary's actions in John 12 in a different light?

2. At first glance, Judas's question in 12:5 seems like a good one. But Mary's act was an act of love and worship. How do differing views of what is good or right still trip Christians up today?

3. What does this short passage tell us about Judas?

4. Why would Jesus keep such close company to someone like Judas?

5. Mary and Martha were upset that Jesus had not come in time to save their brother, Lazarus, from dying. But He raised Lazarus from the dead. What would have changed if Jesus healed Lazarus from sickness instead of raising him from the dead? How is this resurrection different from/like the resurrection of Christ?

Read John 12:12-19

1. Jesus' is gaining more and more popularity. How is that demonstrated in this passage?

2. The Pharisees are becoming increasingly frustrated with Jesus' popularity. What is driving their anger toward Him?

3. Many of the people at this makeshift parade are there because they are curious. They've heard that Jesus raised Lazarus from the dead. What brings people to Christ today?

4. Does Jesus still perform miracles today? If so, name some.

5. What part do we play in the miracles of Christ?

Read John 16:16-33

1. In verse 20 Jesus tells His disciples, "You will weep and mourn while the world rejoices. You will grieve, but your grief will turn to joy." What is He referring to?

2. Jesus talks about complete joy that cannot be taken away (v. 22). What is the difference between joy and happiness?

3. What things get in the way of your promise of complete joy? How can you maintain joy in a world like this?

4. In the Old Testament, people talked to God through a priest. How has the relationship between God (the Father) and the believer changed because of Jesus (vv. 23-24)?

5. The final verse of this passage can offer much comfort to a Christian. What in verse 33 gives you the greatest joy?

Closing Thoughts

What have you learned in this study that seems the most significant or meaningful to you?

Closing Prayer

As a group, close in prayer, thanking God for what you have learned during this session. Ask Him to continue to speak to you; promise to listen.

2
The Last Supper
John 13:1–38

Prayer

Begin your Bible study with a brief prayer. Ask God to open your hearts and to help you understand His Word.

Opening Thoughts

Dinner with friends. Sounds good, right? But think about what Jesus is facing over the course of a meal. His "to-do" list might look something like this:

- Wash feet and teach about service.
- Answer questions.
- Announce Judas's betrayal.
- Answer more questions.
- Tell friends good-bye.
- Answer still more questions.
- Predict Peter's denial.
- Prepare for trial, incredible pain, and crucifixion.

Although the scriptural account of this supper isn't lengthy, what is done and said at this meal is key. And you can be sure that to Jesus, it was a lot more than just a simple dinner with friends.

Discuss the Scripture

Read John 13:1-20

1. What distinction between temptation and sin are you able to discover in verse 2?

2. In dry weather, the roads of Palestine would be inches deep in dust. In wet weather, they would turn to liquid mud. Sandals were worn. Upon arrival at a home, someone would wash the feet of others. How do you think Judas felt as Jesus washed his feet? How do you think you would have felt?

3. What do we learn about being a servant in this passage? Is it harder for you to be a servant or to have someone serve you? Why?

4. What are some specific ways you can become a servant?

5. In what ways is verse 17 both a responsibility and a gift?

Read John 13:21-30

1. What does verse 21 remind us about Jesus?

2. Why do you think Jesus doesn't come right out and name Judas as the one who would betray Him?

3. What do you think scared the disciples most, the knowledge that Jesus would be betrayed or the knowledge that the betrayal came from one of their own?

4. Read Luke 22:1-6. What motivated Judas to betray Jesus?

5. Is money still a motive for betrayal today? Give some examples of how lives are destroyed for love of money.

Read John 13:31-38

1. What did Jesus consider as glory (12:23-28, 31-32)? What do people count as glory today?

2. Why would Jesus' news in 13:33 be surprising to the disciples? Why would it be frightening?

3. Jesus gives His disciples a new command to love one another in verse 34. Why is this command new in light of what has just happened and in light of what will soon be happening?

4. After Peter's claim in verse 37, why was it important for Jesus to warn him as He did in verse 38?

5. Have you ever felt a warning from the Lord? If you are willing, share it with the group.

Closing Thoughts

What have you learned in this study that seems the most significant or meaningful to you?

Closing Prayer

As a group, close in prayer, thanking God for what you have learned during this session. Ask Him to continue to speak to you; promise to listen.

3

A Friend Is Coming
John 14:15-31; 16:5-15

Prayer

Begin your Bible study with a brief prayer. Ask God to open your hearts and to help you understand His Word.

Opening Thoughts

Although the disciples had been told they could trust in Christ when their hearts were troubled, although they had been given the promise of heaven, although they were now able to speak to the Father directly because of Christ, there was still something bothering them. They were worried by the news that their Shepherd was leaving. The question plagued them—How do you follow a man after death has taken Him from you? Jesus was prepared to give them an answer, to give them help, to promise them the Holy Spirit. He would also show them the way to where He was going—to the Father—via suffering, death, and resurrection.

The role of the Holy Spirit would be essential following the departure of Jesus, because by way of the Holy Spirit, Jesus would come to them, be known by them, and remind them of His words. The Holy Spirit is the Spirit of the Resurrected Jesus. We know this because after all the explanation of the Comforter, Jesus simply says, "I will come to you" (John 14:18).

Discuss the Scripture

Read John 14:15-31

1. Jesus seems to offer three keys to the disciple so that this promised spiritual power can operate. Identify them (Key One: vv. 13-14, Key Two: v. 15, Key Three: vv. 16-17).

2. What advantage does the Spirit's relationship with the disciples have over Christ's relationship with them while on earth (v. 16)?

3. In verse 17, Jesus tells His disciples that they already know the Holy Spirit. How can this be so?

4. What two names are given to the Holy Spirit in verses 16 and 17? What do these names tell us about the Holy Spirit and the nature of our relationship with Him? In what way are Jesus and the Holy Spirit one?

5. What enables believers to obey Christ (vv. 15, 21, 23)?

6. What does Jesus mean when He says, "I do not give to you as the world gives" (v. 27)? How does the world give?

7. The Holy Spirit is not the only thing Jesus promises to leave His followers. What promise does He make in verse 27?

8. Jesus' words about the Holy Spirit in v. 17 say, "He lives with you and will be in you." Jesus is promising His disciples a deeper relationship with the Spirit. They already had a relationship with the Spirit by knowing Jesus (see 1:32). But a deeper experience with the Spirit was still to come.

On the Day of Pentecost Jesus' promise was kept. The disciples were filled with the Spirit (Acts 2:4), and a new age dawned—the age of the Spirit.

Today, all who have accepted Christ have the Spirit (Rom. 8:9); they have been "born of . . . the Spirit" (John 3:5). However, like the disciples, they can also expect to experience the Spirit in a deeper way (see Eph. 3:14-21). If we have been "born of the Spirit," we still need to be "filled with the Spirit."

How deep is your relationship with the Holy Spirit today? If you have been filled with the Spirit, describe how this experience changed your life.

Read John 16:5-15

1. Jesus spoke repeatedly of His Father as "him who sent me" (v. 5). How does His sense of mission affect me today (see John 17:17-18)?

15

2. In 16:5-7 the disciples seemed more concerned about what would happen to them than what was happening to Christ. Jesus reminds them that there is a benefit for them in His leaving. What is it?

3. Have you ever tried to convict a person that he or she is sinning? What was the result? Why is it better to have the Holy Spirit convict people of their sin (vv. 8-10)?

4. Where would we be without the Holy Spirit who was sent to convict the world of sin?

5. Verse 13 says that the Holy Spirit not only convicts us but also guides us. What is our responsibility when we feel the Holy Spirit's guiding? If you are willing, tell of a time when the Holy Spirit convicted you or guided you.

6. How does this passage help us to better understand the relationship between the God the Father, Jesus the Son, and the Holy Spirit?

Closing Thoughts

What have you learned in this study that seems the most significant or meaningful to you?

Closing Prayer

As a group, close in prayer, thanking God for what you have learned during this session. Ask Him to continue to speak to you; promise to listen.

4

Jesus Prays
John 17:1–26

Prayer

Begin your Bible study with a brief prayer. Ask God to open your hearts and to help you understand His Word.

Opening Thoughts

After intensive instruction to the disciples to prepare them for His leaving, Jesus goes further. He prays for them because so much is at stake—their spiritual progress and the future of the Kingdom.

This chapter 17, called the "high-priestly prayer," is the longest recorded prayer of Jesus. It is no gloomy, desperate prayer; rather it has a sense of victory. It is prayed by the One who has "overcome the world" (16:33). The prayer is comprised of three parts: in verses 1-5 Jesus prays for himself, in verses 6-19 Jesus prays for His disciples, and in verses 20-26 Jesus prays for future disciples. In verse 20 Jesus said, "My prayer is not for them alone. I pray also for those who will believe in me through their message." In other words, Jesus prayed the last part of this prayer with you in mind.

Discuss the Scripture

Read John 17:1-5

1. The glory of God is the revelation of His character and presence. To glorify God means to give honor or praise to Him. How had Christ glorified the Father (v. 4)? How would the Father glorify Christ (v. 5)?

2. If we understand that Christ's glory included the Cross, what was He asking for in verses 1 and 5?

3. In what ways may we glorify God?

4. What is Jesus' definition of eternal life (v. 3)?

Read John 17:6-19

1. Make a list of words that could be used to describe the disciples' spirituality as Jesus describes them in this passage.

2. How many of those words could you use to describe your own spirituality?

3. Jesus' leaving would be a great shock to the disciples. He especially prayed that they would be protected or kept. What or whom did they need protection from (vv. 12-15)?

4. Read verses 14 and 15 again. What does it mean to be in the world but not of the world?

5. What does Jesus ask His Father to do for the disciples as the climactic fulfillment of all His other requests for them (v. 17)? As you understand it, what does it mean for God to sanctify a Christian?

Read John 17:20-26

1. How do we know that the prayer for disciples in verses 6-19 applies to us also (v. 20)?

2. What does it mean to be one or to have complete unity (v. 21)?

3. What things keep us as Christ's disciples from experiencing complete unity? How are sanctification and unity related?

4. What does Jesus say He wants in verse 24? How does this affect your relationship with Him?

5. When Jesus went back to heaven to be with His Father, His work was not done. What is Jesus' continuing work (v. 26)?

Closing Thoughts

What have you learned in this study that seems the most significant or meaningful to you?

Closing Prayer

As a group, close in prayer, thanking God for what you have learned during this session. Ask Him to continue to speak to you; promise to listen.

5

The Darkest Hour
John 18 and 19

Prayer

Begin your Bible study with a brief prayer. Ask God to open your hearts and to help you understand His Word.

Opening Thoughts

In these two chapters of John, Jesus must face not only friends who betray and deny Him but also an excruciating death. Crucifixion was a cruel, painful death usually reserved for conquered enemies, slaves, or criminals. The persons who gathered around Him while He died probably didn't understand yet that He was taking their place. But in His death on the Cross, Jesus identified with the least, the last, and the lost. He even died for the very people who were crucifying Him.

Discuss the Scripture

Read John 18:1-27

1. What was Jesus' way of facing the most difficult moment of His life (v. 1)? How often is that your first response in your difficult times?

2. Jesus clearly identified himself twice as the One whom the arresting officials were looking for (vv. 4-8). What was He concerned about (vv. 8-9)?

3. In verse 10 Simon Peter makes a bold move to save his beloved Jesus. We've seen Jesus with a money-loving betrayer and now with a person who is confrontational and violent. Do these types of people have a place in the kingdom of God? How are we to react to such personalities?

4. In this passage, Peter moves from trying to protect Jesus to denying that he even knows Him (v. 17). What do you think brings about this change in Peter?

5. What new things can we learn about Jesus' character from His response to being arrested and from His responses at His trial?

Read John 18:28—John 19:16

1. In what ways did Pilate attempt to deal with making a decision about the fate of Jesus? Whose side is Pilate on?

2. What did Jesus say was His purpose in coming to Earth (18:37)?

3. How is His purpose ironic considering why He is being put to death (19:7)?

4. In v. 10, Pilate told Jesus that he had power over Him. How did Jesus react to this threat? What is the difference between Jesus' power and Pilate's power?

5. What fear of Pilate's did the Jews use to get Jesus crucified (v. 12)? How may one's personal ambition determine his or her conduct in a moral crisis?

Read John 19:17-42

1. How was Christ's suffering on the Cross different from the suffering of the two thieves crucified with Him?

2. Read Isa. 53:5-6. What does this tell us about Christ's death on the Cross?

3. What do you think the soldiers' gambling for Christ's garment beneath the Cross tells us about typical human attitudes or values (John 19:23)?

4. How did Jesus express concern for His mother in verses 26-27? What does this teach us about Jesus' character?

5. Read verse 30 again. What does Jesus mean when He says, "It is finished"? Also, what does it mean that Jesus "gave up his spirit"?

Closing Thoughts
What have you learned in this study that seems the most significant or meaningful to you?

Closing Prayer
As a group, close in prayer, thanking God for what you have learned during this session. Ask Him to continue to speak to you; promise to listen.

6

The Brightest Dawn
John 20 and 21

Prayer

Begin your Bible study with a brief prayer. Ask God to open your hearts and to help you understand His Word.

Opening Thoughts

After Christ's death on the Cross, two followers lovingly placed Jesus' body in a tomb. This was on Friday. Early Sunday morning, Mary Magdalene discovered that the stone that had sealed the entrance to the tomb was gone. What follows is a beautiful story of resurrection, reappearance, and recognition.

In a sense John's Gospel could have ended with chapter 20. But chapter 21 tells the story of the restoration of Peter following the denial of Jesus. To leave the leader of the church hanging in midair would have left some serious unfinished business. Where chapter 20 is the joyful resurrection of Christ, the ultimate glorification of God's power and promise, chapter 21 is almost the opposite. It could have been titled "Back to Life as Normal (Where Broken Things Need Repair)." Depicted are such ordinary matters as a day at work, a breakfast meeting, and a much-needed conversation between friends. In these last two chapters of John, watch how Christ moves from the Cross, to the tomb, to houses of friends, and out into the world.

Discuss the Scripture

Read John 20:1-18

1. When Mary, Peter, and John discover an empty tomb, they are distressed instead of joyful (vv. 1-9). Why?

2. Why does Jesus say, "*Who* is it you are looking for?" (v. 15) instead of "*What* is it you are looking for?" Have you ever gone to God seeking a "what" or "why" when you should have been seeking a "who"? If you are willing, share that experience.

3. Read John 10:3-4. What finally caused Mary to recognize Jesus (20:16)? What does this tell you about their relationship?

4. Can you think of a time when Jesus was present with you, but it took you awhile to recognize Him? How did you finally know it was Jesus?

5. What conclusion do you make about God's priorities when you realize that Christ's first reappearance was to Mary Magdalene?

Read John 20:19-31

1. Jesus appears to the disciples behind locked doors. Why are the doors locked and what does this have to do with the way Jesus greets His followers (v. 19)?

2. In verses 20 and 21 Jesus follows a common pattern. He gives the disciples both a responsibility and a gift. What is the responsibility? What is the gift?

3. Are you continually receiving the gift? Are you continually taking up the responsibility?

4. Thomas, often called doubting Thomas, is another interesting personality (vv. 24-25). Why is it harder for some people to believe than others?

5. Through this study, you've come to know people like Mary, Martha, Peter, and Thomas. Discuss their unique personalities briefly. Which person are you most like and how does his or her interactions with Christ help you in your own relationship with Him?

Read John 21

1. When Jesus appears to the disciples in the beginning of chapter 21, how is this time different from His earlier reappearances?

2. What is the special reason that Jesus calls Peter "Simon son of John" in 21:15 when in John 1:42, He had said he would be called Peter, a rock? Why might Jesus ask Peter if he loves Him three times? Can you think of another thing that occurred three times? How do these two relate?

3. Peter had once boldly proclaimed, "Even if all fall away on account of you, I never will" (Matt. 26:33). What did Peter now have to admit? Can you recall a personal experience when Christ had to break down a self-sufficient attitude in you? If you are willing, share this experience with the group.

4. In John 21:15 what is Jesus referring to when He asks Peter if he loves Him "more than these"? How does the restoration of Simon Peter to a position of leadership inform our restoration of those who fall?

5. In this last chapter of John, what commands does Jesus give His disciples on how they are to proceed in ministry (vv. 16, 19, 22)? What commands might He be giving to you?

Closing Thoughts

What have you learned in this study that seems the most significant or meaningful to you?

Closing Prayer

As a group, close in prayer, thanking God for what you have learned during this session. Ask Him to continue to speak to you; promise to listen.

www.ingramcontent.com/pod-product-compliance
Lightning Source LLC
Chambersburg PA
CBHW060548030426
42337CB00021B/4490